BULLSHIT FREE SALES MANAGEMENT

----- & -----

THE CRESCENDO SALES PITCH STRATEGY

Dedication

Thanks to all the sales professionals I have had the privilege of working with. I can't say it's all been fun, but we've made a lot of money and had some great laughs.

Thanks to Pat Fogle who kept me on track throughout the writing process and read every word... multiple times. Thanks to Angelique Martin's words to live by; *"I don't try anything... I just do it!"* And thanks to Parker Belle, Bishop, and Asher for putting up with a wildman for a father in a crazy profession. I love all you guys.

Table of Contents

Prologue 1

Part 1: Bullshit Free Sales Management 5

Chapter 1: Why Sales Managers /Directors Fail 7

Chapter 2: Managing Your Team 28

Chapter 3: The Rep Curve Balls And Traps 41

Chapter 4: Curve Balls And Traps From Your Founder/ Ceo /Vps 50

Chapter 5: Rep Sales Styles 55

Chapter 6: The Poisoned Well Syndrome 63

Chapter 7: Hiring A Sales Team / Human Resources 67

Chapter 8: Clearly Defining A "Lead", From A "Suspect" To A "Prospect" 78

Part 2: The Crescendo Pitch Strategy 87

Prologue

Sales is a craft, plain and simple. It takes just as much time and effort to master this craft as it would to be a carpenter, a surgeon, an attorney, or a painter. The higher your mastery, the more accomplished you are in achieving your goals; you make more money, you're able to convince others... whatever you feel this mastery offers.

In some circles, sales is frowned upon as a lesser profession. This is probably the results of numerous commercials and movies depicting the slimy car salesman (with a lime green suit and large collared shirt) unscrupulously selling a bad product with a sweaty smile on their faces... Sure, those people are out there. I've met them (and even sold to them...), but they aren't the majority. They are, by far, the minority.

Like anything, you become what you put into it. There are good doctors and there are bad ones, just as with any profession. You are responsible for the level of your craft and the direction you take your mastery. The hope is that this book and a little self-reflection will help you get you closer to that mastery.

It's funny, when you're interviewing for a sales position or sales manager, the questions don't actually focus on sales craft. They might discuss your sales results (which can be influenced by numerous factors; pre-existing sales relationships, marketing automation, market share, being there at the right time...), but you never really discuss your sales approach and how one responds to certain situations and personnel scenarios. I think that, most of the time, the person doing the interview hasn't worked in the sales role and believes there's some mystical reason for your success.

I also have a small belief that human resources personnel look upon sales professionals with a skeptical (maybe even negative) eye. Possibly because they feel that this sales professional is more likely to manipulate them throughout the hiring process. That, or they carry the thought that salespeople are a disposable and plentiful commodity, or something that can be replaced with Artificial Intelligence or a CRM's marketing automation.

The truth of how this book came about is from my experience as a sales director in the field. I began to notice that sales professionals in the market didn't know what their profession actually was. They knew they were a "Account Executive", because that's what's on their business card and that's what they interviewed for, but they had no clue what it entailed. That and their managers had no time or had been so far removed from sales that they'd lost the skill or taste for the actual work.

A lot of the times when I would go into these markets, I would see these brand new sales professionals sitting in front of a computer or television screen for hours watching a 1990's sales training program. These new sales executives' first experience would be a talking head in a late 80s suit with permed hair waxing poetic about his smooth tactics while making cheesy jokes. This is not how sales training should be executed - and certainly the wrong approach to giving new sales professionals an accurate depiction of their future role.

That's why in Part 2 of this book I added "The Crescendo Sales Pitch Tactic", which will hopefully help your newer reps understand what their role is and more importantly how to go about it properly.

I've written this little book in a fashion that is easy to understand and share. And that's exactly the point. I cover more of the "soft skills" needed for your day-to-day management of your team that are not usually covered in training courses. I want you to see problems or challenging scenarios before they happen, versus falling into inefficient time sucks that will tax you and the team's success.

Trust me when I say that I've sat in numerous "sales training" courses where an outside consultant explores scenarios for niche business verticals which you or your sales professionals either won't ever work with. This, again, is worthless. Lots of talk that converts to noise which converts to a waste of time.

Let's cut out all that shit and just get on with it. You've chosen to read this book to gain knowledge and build professional mastery, so let's go.

Part 1

Chapter 1

Why Sales Managers /Directors Fail

There are few jobs in the corporate hierarchy that have a more tangible responsibility and direct impact on a company's bottom line than a sales manager/director. This is because no other departments or titles touch every aspect of the company. From accounting and legal to customer service, you and your sales team are involved. This is unique; unlike other departments, where their roles and responsibilities are fairly linear or black and white, yours lives in the world of gray. I do give credit to the human resources departments, but more often than not they're just handing their responsibilities and headaches over to you. Thus, you are accountable for everything.

You are accountable for the hiring and firing, the training, the managing, selling, pricing, marketing, budgeting, reporting, every little billing issue and customer service quibble for your company... It's all your responsibility and, if something goes wrong at any moment... well, you have to be ready to wade in. With all of this responsibility laid upon you, it's inevitable that you'll be questioned or blamed for something, real or not. This is why the average tenure for a sales manager/director now is 19 months. That's pretty shocking, not to mention unfortunate. This book will help to navigate some of this unhealthy churn, but not all. You will fall on your sword and/or be beheaded in due time. It's the nature of the job.

This again goes back to the volatility of the role. It's nearly impossible to keep everything under control. Here are the reasons for your demise or high turnover:

Pre-existing Conditions with the Founder/CEO:

Numerous times I have walked into a new company role knowing from the outset that there were some pre-existing issues that needed cleaning up. Unfortunately, you come to realize that those conditions are permanent company fixtures that will not be fixed. These conditions often include a company founder/CEO/VP who is a narcissistic, controlling sociopath that has completely unrealistic expectations for you and your team, and/or enjoys the thrill and control of creating chaos. They start companies just to have people worship them or because they have personalities that are so toxic that they had no friends to begin with (and their families are happy to see them leave every day). These people truly do exist in the corporate world. At times, you won't see it until you're six weeks into your position. Unfortunately, there's not much you can do in this situation apart from quit or put your head down until another opportunity comes along.

I always stress that you need to look deeply into company review websites and BBB; do a pros and cons reflection prior to accepting your position with a new company. A little due diligence will go a long way to saving both your sanity and hair – nobody wants to go gray early. Trust me, I've taken roles for big salaries and titles only to wish I'd never heard of it.

The health of the company comes from the top (it sounds cliché, but it's true). They can have a thousand happy hours, rah-rah company outings, and cafeterias stocked deep with the most non-GMO, BPA, gluten-free, grass-fed, organic, reef-safe snacks, but if the head of your company is a bi-polar tyrant, then it's impossible to keep things positive and moving forward.

Conflicting Direction(s):

There will be times as a manager where there are two or more conflicting ideas on how your team should be run, how a strategy should be executed, or the true reality of a problem. Examples of this include;

1) You are unable to hire new reps because the pay is lower than market/industry standards and you are asking for more
2) Setting unrealistic budgetary goals (this happens often)
3) Unrealistic KPIs or Key Process Indicators (we'll discuss the positives and negatives to CRMs)
4) How and why to structure a sales team...

Despite the fact that the people who run and/or take over companies are generally intelligent and responsible for making things happen within their companies, this doesn't mean that they have had any experience in sales or running a sales team. Thus, their opinion(s) on your department and its parts and pieces can be challenging, if challenged.

A prime example of this was when the owner of a company was diligently harping on at myself and my team about why we weren't using the historical client database to generate new sales. He came from a software development background, so he knew the power of leveraging data and was very irritated that this opportunity wasn't being acted upon by myself and the sales team.

What he didn't understand was how the content of the database was collected. He did not understand why or how the files were corrupted with incomplete data and/or suffered from massive contact duplications (disclaimer: all these things happened before I got there). It really didn't help with his frustration when I purged the errors from the database, only to see it was a tenth of the size of what he originally thought. I suspected that he thought he was sitting on a goldmine of new opportunities. He wasn't. This caused him a great deal of frustration which spewed out in the form of an excessive amounts of emails, late night calls, and contested dialogue, all of which became a problem and made for a bad day at the office for me.

He was a programmer by nature and profession. He struggled to understand that there were nuances to sales that weren't black and white numbers.

Sales and running sales departments are both messy activities. Your duty is to manage everyone's expectations of not only the real, but also the subjective and fantasy.

Being Submarined (Undermined):

As much as you might want to steer away from toxic elements, people, and/or scenarios, you wouldn't be doing your job if you didn't ruffle someone's feathers, directly or indirectly. Unfortunately, this might cause blowback in the form of being undermined by a co-worker, manager, or subordinate. This usually happens when someone either wants your job, doesn't like you or your management styles and policies, or is just intimidated by you. Many times you will be forced to defend yourself, an individual, or your team over the most ludicrous things... like being successful at your role.

I have worked side-by-side with another manager in my role who wasn't as successful at turning around the personnel on their team and was infuriated that I could get mine to perform or hit that elusive goal. Through that frustration of possibly looking bad, they will in turn try to make you look bad. You see this a lot in competing departments or regions where they're always looking for angles or traps to make you look bad. It's a challenging scenario, but it happens every day. The bigger the salary and role, the higher the stakes.

Believe it or not, I've asked sales managers and sales teams to read business-specific articles and books (these weren't long academic passages, typically short and easy books like this one) with the intent of helping them overcome a current gap in their sales craft. Pretty simple, right? Only later I'd hear from the CEO that he didn't want anyone "reading" from here on out because one or two of the sales reps had complained, to which he stated he would work it out with me.

Sooooooo... here's a double-dipped undermining situation (which, on reflection, is all pretty laughable, really). One of the reps (an underperformer) goes around you to complain to the CEO in a "tell on Mom to Dad" situation. Then the CEO backs-up the rep and undermines your authority and direction while discrediting your time and efforts.

So later in the year, when the CEO tells you and the head of HR that we need to hire sales reps that are more mature and of a higher caliber (note: but is unwilling to pay for that experience), you can look at him blankly as you scream in horror on the inside (see the *pre-existing conditions with CEO* section for reference).

Again, non-sales personnel or departments can sometimes look at sales as a necessary evil - as the people who make an absorbent amount of money or are with the loudest department down the hall (the occasional roar of laughter doesn't help). They can be looked upon as an unwanted foreign entity. You need to be aware of this and ready to joust and fence when questions or scenarios like these arise.

Again, this is the reality of your job. There are plenty of feel-good sugar-coated bullshit sales manager books out there. This is not one of them.

I'm here to help.

Not Meeting Budget:

This is actually one that's pretty cut and dry. If you aren't meeting a budget and there are no solutions coming from you, it's going to be a struggle. Missing the budget can be because of:

- Old or non-relevant products or services

This can be a tough one. I worked in media sales for about 7 years and when I first started at a local television station, the only competitors were the other stations in the area. Upon the proliferation of broadband and the mass adoption of mobile devices (Apple introduced the iPhone in 2007, followed by HTC G1 Android phones in 2008), viewership started to fall generously year after year. This, in turn, made broadcast television commercials harder to sell.

The downward progression of viewers left upper management slow to react to - or even come to terms with at all - the fact that their 100-year reign of media supremacy was falling apart on their watch. The once cash-cow was struggling. Our product was losing relevance and seemed old and cumbersome. These were challenges that we could handle in the beginning, but as streaming technology (YouTube and Netflix) began to take root, the viewers began to check out. Our sales followed.

Before you decide to take on a new role, it's important to know where that product and company stands in the marketplace. You don't want to be holding the bag and trying to make water into wine. It's just not going to happen.

- Product/service pricing and packaging that's out of competitor/market alignment

It's not uncommon for owners of companies or ego-driven leadership to be completely disconnected from the reality of the value(s) of their products. I have seen situations where they have completely out-priced or devalued themselves while questioning why you aren't meeting goals.

The real problem in this scenario is having to convince all those parties that they're wrong. That can be a long and painful course of action.

- Competitor saturation (or you're just getting beat)

These days it's hard to find a company and product that can't be reproduced and duplicated. It's even harder to find a good product that doesn't have a large number of strong competitors.

In SaaS and software, you are continually going up against soooo many competitors in the market that they clog up the communication channel and inundate the prospects with pitches. With so many price/benefit offers, it creates noise. That noise grows to a point that everyone begins to ignore you.

To really have an edge and overcome your competitors, you need to know them and their product as well as you do your own. From there, you can pick them apart.

It's up to you and you team to overcome the noise in the market and set yourself apart.

- Budget lacks diversity (your budget is weighted too heavily on one product)

There have been times where a sales organization's budget was overly weighted to one or two particular clients, verticals, or products; this can be the kiss of death if one of those should go away.

An example of this would be when the local broadcast TV stations focused 60% of their annual sales budgets on the automotive vertical. The lack of diversity bit them when automakers (GM, Ford, Toyota) started seeing consumers gravitating to mobile devices and streaming services and, thus, began moving their advertising dollars into those devices and services.

The broadcast stations didn't have an answer for this problem until later, so it went from 60% to 30%.

- Company reputation and/or historical bad dealings

I've taken on a couple of sales management roles where the companies have had some pre-existing issues with questionable products or procedures. This includes products not doing what they were supposed to do, customer service FUBARs, over-charging the client, and/or a former sales rep completely screwing the customer.

If these are happening under your watch and you are responsible for cleaning up the mess, it makes your job ten times harder. This is because someone had overlooked in the past or just didn't know that this was happening (which is doubtful).

I took over a small sales organization that was selling a truly subpar product. However, they sold a ton because the rep was paid well on the close. The product was so bad that the clients would try to cancel just two weeks into service, but were stuck until the end of the month. They were infuriated and inconsolable. This happened over and over to the point that one prospect would see the caller ID with the company's name and would immediately start screaming at whoever was on the other end of the phone (typically a new sales rep). Those screams began to show up on Google Reviews and Better Business Bureau and Fraud Reports. It wasn't good. I did *not* want to be a part of that, so I killed the product and offered upgrade deals and discounts the following year to the few clients that would accept our apology.

Honesty is the best policy. Don't avoid or deny bad feelings and/or dealings in the past with your customer base. Address it. Fix it. Work to repair the relationship.

- Bad restructure of the team (targeting specific verticals or markets)

When there's a morale problem, there can be both real and fabricated reasons. I've seen situations where the team is upset about how they've been treated on a personal level (having multiple changes in management structure, changes in products, regions, verticals, etc. ...or asking them to read books...). They can interpret these changes as favoritism or punishment.

Some strategies - like having reps focus on certain verticals, regions, and or clients - might sound wonderful on a PowerPoint presentation to the boardroom, but don't actually work. You might be the last one to hear that the strategy is failing and by then it's too late. They're bitter and out of the commissions they might have earned last year.

These changes can look like an enterprise (new sales) team, a key accounts team, a national team, or a specific sale of one or two products.

What happens is everyone wants to be on one team or product because it may seem (or really be) better.

Because there are bigger accounts, more relevant products, fast sales windows, or easier to manage clients... or all the above.

- Changes in a sales team's compensation plan

Here's a great magic trick: do you want to watch the sales team disappear? Screw with their pay. What's bewildering to me is how a company's leadership team thinks that raising a salesperson's budget while paying them less equals a positive result. It takes the same amount of energy to close the account as it did the year before, but now that labor has less value. Again, this is because non-sales people are making decisions without not knowing the reps' market value or what the job entails.

I have also seen this happen when leadership has changed the pricing structure in order to move more units. The true intent was to help the reps. However, this backfired because they were charging less for the product, so the reps were making less per sale (64% less). The reps simply stopped selling and went and found other roles.

- Sales team has become complacent / unmotivated

Sales teams... Sigh... They're just as much as an individual as they are an organization all at the same time. Each team is and should be treated as one every time you take on a new role.

What I mean by this is that I've been brought in on many occasions to "fix" the team. There's a lot that has to happen to "fix" a sales organization; it starts at both the top and the bottom of the organization.

A morale problem can develop for both real and fabricated reasons. I've seen teams upset about how they've been treated on a personal level, but I've also seen teams made up of really, really green reps who don't understand their craft and sales responsibilities.

You will have to define and address specifically what is causing the ailment. More importantly, how you carry yourself (your confidence and positivity) translates to your team. They need someone who's going to inspire them through thick and thin.

- Unforeseen actions, occurrences, economics, or acts of God sway your ability to meet budget

I have worked with some true badass sales directors. Sales operators who consistently overachieved their budgets, their team loved him or her, and was on track for bigger things within the company. But have watched all things go to hell when a massive vendor contract/relationship was negotiated away from his or her team. That contract and its relationship was never a part of their purview, knowledge, or responsibility. It was negotiated by people thousands of miles away who had no knowledge of his and his team's existence. This vendor relationship was worth more than 35% of their total annual sales budget and was tied into numerous sales relationships. They only found out about this loss of the vendor at the beginning of the second quarter. With such late notice, there was no way to recover. It was a devastating blow to them and the team. Leadership needed a scapegoat for the budget losses and the sales director was let go… It was painful for all, not to mention brutal.

Here's a personal one… I lost a thriving business during The Great Recession. I had a young family and poured all my energy into its success, so there was nothing "Great" about the loss. All my business conversations had stalled, followed by a loss of four major client accounts in one month (September 2009). There was absolutely nothing I could do to save them. Many of them went into slow pay cycles or collections.

There was no one to sell to because we were in an economic disaster. It was a painful learning experience.

- The unrealistic and unachievable budget

Yes, I said it! The sometimes unrealistic and unachievable budget… Dah, dah-daaaaaaaaa!

It pains me to bring up this subject, but unfortunately the untouchable budget is a fact of life in the sales management profession. These budgets manifest out of a number of places; the shareholders want to see a big end-of-year return, your boss's boss wants to make a bonus (to buy a yacht), the company is making up for a loss or projected future loss, or - more commonly - the budget comes out of thin air.

I've been under one or two of these ten-ton budgets and they're not fun (I have the gray hair and body count of a good sales rep to prove it). They can add stress and dampen the morale of your team.

Unfortunately, you're going to have to come up with a plan on how to chip away at that budget and save what you can. If your leadership is seeing that you're working hard to come up with a solution, you usually won't get fired (you'll more than likely be verbally beaten-up).

After you and your team (what's left of them) have been killed by one of these, there's usually a learning curve felt by all - along with a feeling of embarrassment. Hopefully this gives leadership a perspective of what is and is not achievable.

Know Who You Work For and Are Working With

Managing a sales team can be anything from the best job in the world to a total mental and physical nightmare.

There have been times where I've managed in roles, my results and team crushed the goal expectations, and they were celebrated and paid accordingly (which was rare). Then there have been numerous times where we've achieved those same spectacular results only to be downtrodden and criticized over subjective opinions.

The difference between the two? Upper management. This included CEOs, CFOs, VPs, and HR.

Sales has always been a "what have you done for me lately..." type of profession with timelines and sales goals. However, if your upper management have never been in a sales role or in sales management... well, now part of your job is in the defensive/education capacity and you'll be busy getting them up to speed. That and along explaining the black and white nature of your current teams results, which are typically open and available to any and all executive team members.

Just for clarification, when I say defensive/education, I mean a number of things that truly stand out from what you might think this role is responsible for. Things like:

- Hiring Practices: Who and how to hire. For some reason, hiring has become a beauty contest where everyone in the room gets an opinion on a candidate. Where HR is asking sales personnel, managers, customer service, CEOs, IT, and anyone else in the building to interview this person and give their opinion... This is a ridiculous effort and the people who go along with this are shortsighted.

- Firing Practices: When it comes to letting someone go because of underperformance or disciplinary issues, again, everyone feels that they need to put in their two cents. This includes HR adding additional work to your load when they should be taking the reins and/or removing themselves completely for all accountability... Or the CEO wants to repurpose this individual in another department because while they're incompetent, they are "a good guy" or funny or, more likely, attractive...

- Sales Training: Again and again I've seen a top tier executive get sold on a sales training concept while totally failing to understand the material and concepts. And again and again I have watched active sales teams sit through week-long sessions with well-paid instructors (typically with little or no sales experience) who lay out sales question scenarios and beautiful posters of how their sales theory should go. Each time this happens, the company follows the theories and path, but slowly realizes that most (if not all) are either not applicable or straight-up hokey.

- Confusing Marketing and Sales: At times, you are drawn into the discussion or have to draw a line regarding the marketing department's responsibilities. This line in the sand happens a lot when it comes to the marketing of your company and its products. It's your responsibility to give feedback to the marketing team on what you're hearing in the field, as well as what tools are needed to make your sales team more successful. That's it. However, at times marketing heads feel it's necessary to voice how your team should engage prospects or clients, or maybe share their concerns about sales trends. This counter-productive feedback should be nipped in the bud early and often, as this storyline can later manifest as the marketing department's excuse for their incompetence to gain marketing traction or do anything substantial.

- Sales Perks or Trips: When it comes to offering your sales personnel quarterly or end-of-year goal bonuses, you have to be part of the education process for all non-sales parties. Part of this is letting them understand that sales personnel are not motivated by the same things other departments might be… However, for whatever reason, it seems at times that Marketing, HR, or the Head of Accounting will toss in their idea of what should be a "Great!" sales perk or goal. A gift card to a chain restaurant, a piece of cheap technology, tickets to the losing team's weekday game, a weekend getaway to a venue that's in the off-season… all these ideas fall on deaf ears and create animosity within the sales team. You know what motivates them (or at least, you should), so you should be the one that defines great perks.

- Sales Commissions: This one really, really matters. Sales commissions and bonus tiers are what define success and happiness within sales organizations. You can add cafeterias, happy hours, summer hours, pets in the office, and group outings (which are all great), but that's to entice and sustain the headcount. Plain and simple, sales personnel are motivated by money. The bigger the money, the more their motivation, the greater the team's success. However, this concept is lost if and when CFOs, accounting departments, and HR get involved. They see money as a micromanaged line item or are looking for economic social justice throughout the entire company. They might see salespeople as an exorbitant large expense. Those departments and personalities fail to understand what's involved in flushing out suspects, bringing in prospects, and selling them to be a client. They fail to see that sales drives the company's overall success. Numerous times I have built a budget and pay plan that's fair and pays based on results, but when the CFO, accounting department head, or HR start reviewing a sales rep's yearly commissions, they state that this is too much. Now you're responsible for fighting it out over why it isn't based on that rep's yield in sales… This is a very contentious scenario which becomes extremely heated, particularly when this rep is making twice the salary of the accounting department or HR head. Thus the reason these parties need to be totally removed from the conversation and process, if and when possible.

It should be duly noted that everyone in a department typically has the company's best interests at hand and just wants to help and make an impact. Everyone wants to be a part of the pointed part of the spear. Sales is usually on the move, vocal (loud), and with outgoing (codeword for wild) personalities to boot. It gets it. However, you have to be clear that they have other responsibilities.

*** One last point: If you allow others to dictate or implement outside ideas that affect your team without your influence or buy-in, you have lost control of your role and the direction of the team. What's lost is hard to bring back. I have watched numerous organizations implement radical changes to commission structures only to see the company lose all its strong sales personnel while sales benchmarks begin to crash. All the while, you're holding the bag and having to explain that it was their decision a year ago to scale back commissions.

Scary stuff. But this is what you signed up for. It's fun!

Chapter 2

Managing Your Team

Now that I've scared the living shit out of you or caused you to reconsider your current professional career, let's discuss the actual job you were hired for; managing your sales team.

Keeping On Their Toes

As a sales manager, you wear numerous hats over a regular work week. However, your role is very simple: to **lead**. This doesn't mean being a taskmaster who beats their team into submission, nor should you handle everyone with kid gloves while doing all the work for them. It's a blend of both while strategically looking ahead.

You have to be willing to go to great lengths to support your team - mentally, physically, and financially - while asking them to do the tasks at hand to reach overall success. Plus, you have to do this on an individual basis (this might mean: bailing a top sales rep out of jail, letting them cry as they tell you about their divorce, or helping them navigate through health issues...)

1) Be honest with your own and everyone else's sales numbers

There's one simple truth about your sales: the numbers don't lie. Either you are or are not reaching your sales goal, budgets, or KPIs. After budgets have been built (or dictated), tracking and pacing to that number be simple. If the personnel on your team recognize this and understand the number, there should be no quarrel about the task at hand.

Being clear and upfront with that goal/budget is cut and dry. They are or are not making that number.

If they *are* making the number, work to find ways to help them generate more. This includes adding a cash bonus, time off, sales support in processing paperwork, etc.... (or all of those!)

If they are **not** making the number, your job is to find out why. This is where it gets a little real. You have to be willing to understand the entire human dynamic of where these failures might lie.

Failures include:

1) A disconnect in the amount of effort (or lack thereof) being put forth
2) Putting forth the effort, but focused on the wrong target (audience or business vertical)
3) Lacking the understanding or confidence of how to prospect or handle objections
4) Struggling with their presentations or confidence in presenting
5) Being distracted on the floor
6) All of the above
7) Or they are not the right fit

2) Checking call lists and calls volumes

In a similar fashion to the fact that numbers don't lie, the same goes for generating the right number of outbound calls and building that continued list of new prospects. Making cold calls and sending along emails and text messages are just a part of the job. If there needs to be 100 calls a day to get one sale and it's expected they get one close per day… Well, your rep clearly needs to produce 100 calls. You just have to manage to the expectation of the rep's position.

3) Giving surprise prospect updates

I have never been a fan of "Gotcha" techniques in management. It's just a bad precedent for distrust and deploys a gloom of fear around you. I am, however, open to doing quick and consistent (every day) touch-bases on where things stand in their sales channel.

Just asking: "What does your calendar look like today...?" "How many do you think will close...?"

I ask these questions in stand up meetings, when catching someone in the hall, or just walking through the sales floor... Anywhere and anytime, to the point where everyone on your team should expect the question. Over time, they will begin to tell you before you even have to ask.

A couple of reasons why this works are: A) It clearly defines why we're all here- to make sales. B) It clearly states that their focus should be on where their accounts are and where they are in the channel.

Enforce and sustain the behaviors that are important to the goal.

Constant Training / Support

I cannot say enough about the need to train and support your team.

As the manager or director of the sales organization, it is important that you seek and craft in a poignant and timely fashion. This doesn't mean kicking the can down the road to have an outside "sales training" consultant do the work for you (which I discussed earlier). Or, which might be even worse, is to listen to a manager read off a half-baked or overly broad idea they found on a sales hack website focused on big word counts versus subject matter. As the leader, it's your job to come up with and customize strong points and learnings. Your points and takeaways need to be short, easy to understand, and - more importantly - interesting.

Think about how you can build your team's individual sales craft. Give them the skills they need to be successful.

Here are some training topics:

1) Understanding customer's ROI (aka: the bottoms-up approach)

It's important that your reps know the value of what they're selling to the marketplace and their clients. The best way to achieve this is to show the client their return on investing with your product. In turn, the best way to show this is by asking a couple of simple questions like: what's the worth of one client (net or gross), how many clients or units have you sold now, and how would you like it to be? These client questions help illustrate to both the prospect/client and the reps why your products matter. A return on investment or ROI is a simple risk return analysis.

2) Handling objections

I honestly don't know how this happens, but for some reason handling objections is not discussed in training environments. The main crust of a sales conversation is completely overlooked, where one party (the prospect) tries to throw you and your company off with reasons why they aren't interested in your product. You and your team need to know these objections and their answers or comebacks beforehand to keep them interested in the product and, more importantly, buy something.

It's not uncommon for me to walk into our Monday morning sales meeting, ask a rep to stand up, and ask them three responses to objections. I then have the team grade those responses and write down the best one.

Client objections like:

Objection: *"It's not in my budget."*
Rep Response: *"Funny you should mention that, we just rolled a monthly pay plan or a couple of great financing options..."*

Objection: *"I'm happy with our current vendor..."*
Rep Response: *"I get it, that's a cool product/company. We have a number of clients that merged over from _____ because we (enter in cheaper, are faster, are better) and have had far better success for it. Let me show you a quick demo..."*

Etc., etc....

You and your sales team should be cataloging and rattling off responses in their sleep. That's their job.

3) Using the correct pitch language and phrasing

One thing you have to realize is that new sales personnel don't understand that they must learn to master *Sales Craft*. They don't get that they should develop the skills of persuasion and confidence while using language and it's phrasing.

As a manager, it's your responsibility to understand what's coming out of every rep's mouth. Are they saying the right thing? Are they being too negative? Are they rolling over too quickly? And are they making the conversation too complicated?

Today, one of the tasks I ask my reps to do in front of the group is explain a product or service in the simplest fashion. I say, *"Explain XYZ to me as if I were your parent, who had no background or knowledge in our industry..."* I then ask them to do this with their prospects or clients. Make things simple. It asks them to practice the KISS theory (keep it simple, stupid).

4) Grammatical errors in business emails and text messages

To my horror, I have read such bad rep correspondences (emails and texts) that were so uninterpretable, one might question if it was written in a drunken blur. Phonics, slang, and pop culture phrasing replaced comprehensible sentences and paragraphs.

In any business environment, this is truly unacceptable. However, it can also be challenging addressing this type of error(s) with the person who wrote it. I understand that there might be gaps between one sales rep's writing ability to the next, but you have to come up with ways to guarantee your prospects and customers are being communicated with correctly.

Some of the items you need to pay attention to beyond tone, spelling, and grammatical errors (which can, to a certain extent, be alleviated with writing software) are the technical aspects of their email signatures and support images that accompany them (I have seen headshots that looked more appropriate on dating sites versus business emails.)

5) Roleplay

Monday mornings (or any morning) can be a struggle in terms of getting your team awake, up to speed, and with the juices flowing. One good way to do this is surprise roleplay.

When roleplaying, you want to make it a pertinent activity that helps to sharpen the skills of day-to-day scenarios. These can include handling common objections, best openings to a cold call, explaining products/service benefits, explaining a competitor's faults, etc.

6) Pitching your peers (any product in front of the group)

Another tried-and-true skills training tactic for your team is to ask them to present a product, service, or belief to the rest of the team. This can be any item they want, they just have to do it in a comprehensive, deliberate, and persuasive fashion.

I asked them to do it with an audience, usually with a PowerPoint presentation with product samples and props.

A couple of things happen over time doing these "Peer Pitches". First, your reps become more confident and smoother (especially the newer reps). Then they begin to better understand that sales is a craft and start to internalize what it takes to gain mastery of their profession.

7) How to prospect

Prospecting is half the battle when it comes to enterprise sales. It can be a struggle for even the most advanced sales reps. Working with your team on a regular basis on where to source prospect names and numbers is always a rewarding exercise. It shows your willingness to understand the daily struggle of prospect outreach and show the team that you're invested in their overall success.

Your reps will be approached by prospect sources like business intelligence software providers and list aggregators. It will be particularly important to vet which provider will give you the best possible service and value for your group.

8) Nonverbal skills

These are broad subjects, but they're always ones to revisit again and again over time. If you're paying attention to the feedback and questions during each training, you hear other areas that might need enlightenment.

* Sidenote on training: Everyone learns in different ways: tactically (by doing), verbally or listening, and/or visually. You need to make sure that you're covering all three bases when you're training your personnel. It should also be noted that people have the tendency to not ask questions in a group environment, so it's important to circle back around to each individual to check for their understanding of the subject matter. When you do this, the sales person has the ability to reflect and/or respond in their own words and without the judgement of their peers.

** Second sidenote: Please know your subject matter. Don't go into a training session without fully understanding the material or subject. If you have a true sales team, they can smell blood in the water and will tear you up. You will thus lose credibility. Be prepared for their questions (real and not), jokes, jaunts, and rolling of the eyes… Be prepared to counter and answer.

Have fun with it. Inject humor, when necessary and often.

However, training is also where I see managers continually fail. This means one of three things: 1) They don't think about their role enough, nor how to better develop their personnel and increase the team's overall effectiveness. 2) They're neither ready nor mature enough to completely fit the role. 3) They have alternative motivations to be in the role.

Where do you stand?

Point number three is a sticking point with me because I think this is the main reason sales organizations flounder or fail in the long-run. This is because people are sometimes put in management roles in which they are not competent. Many times I've seen subordinates put in positions of management by attrition of staff (that last person that hasn't quit or been fired), they are experts in "Managing Up" (code for kissing the bosses' asses), or beg, cajole, or bully their way into getting the title. To many, that is the only thing that matters; the title and/or prospect of an increased salary (who could blame them).

The unfortunate thing about these people is they're great at taking and dispensing orders*, but do so in a horrible fashion. When this happens, they beat down the sales personnel - which then directly affects overall sales.

* Please note that I'm not saying that managers should act as rogue individuals by countering every directive handed down via executive orders. I'm saying that a part of a manager's role is to devise tactics and scenarios to deliver news or protocols to the team. It's your job to look at the tone and timing of the delivery of those protocols. You need to be clear with your executive team on any concerns and suggest alternatives on how it could and can be positioned. It's not time to cower and be silent if there's something that might greatly impact your sales team. Be tactful and clear in your language and points, not insubordinate.

It's important to remember that, at times, the executive staff make decisions that are above your paygrade and may relate to the known or unknown future of the company. That's their role; to make the company thrive and survive. You will become involved in these situations throughout your tenure, like when the company is missing corporate sales projections (regardless of whether or not it's your fault, the heat will be turned up), a corporate buyout (fears of losing jobs), human resource challenges (sexual harassment), and changes in sales compensations (unfortunately this will happen numerous times through your career)... These are all emotionally charged issues that greatly affect the performance dynamics of yourself and your team. Again, it is your role to navigate and lead your team toward the best possible outcome. You bear that burden every day.

Chapter 3

The Rep Curve Balls and Traps

A. Being friends

As a manager or director, you have to walk a fine line between being a responsible human being and doing your job. If you're a good manager, your team should have a strong connection to you and your abilities, meaning your sales team has strong trust in you. At times, this connection can be interpreted as friendship. You need to make it clear that it's not.

Being a good manager should feel like a friendship, but with clear lines of hierarchy and understanding. Meaning you can keep things loose and cordial, but if there are any deviations outside of the responsibilities of the rep (i.e. making the sales/budget), you're going to have to ask hard questions – and, more importantly, strong requests that they need to turn it around.

In my opinion, the "friend versus a manager" problem came into existence during the late 90's and 2000's, when companies and their offices started to relax their formal and sometimes restricting environments. This included deploying open office environments, stocked cafeterias, casual dress codes (versus casual Fridays), and - more recently - "bring your pet to work". All of these changes created the effect of an at-home feel, vibe, and culture. Less stiff and more inviting.

These changes also, however, created an odd and unintended effect. I believe people began to feel so comfortable that their language and interpersonal business relationships became less, well, business-like... I know some HR executive is out there saying; "That's Great! We succeeded in building an emotionally healthy environment for all... it's a working utopia!" However, typically that HR executive isn't dealing with the sales reps madness every day.

We can all have a good laugh and kid around, as I strongly encourage, but if and when things begin to go south, everyone will have to come back down to earth and get the job done.

B. Blaming others

There will be reps that try to blame their lack of results on other sales reps, sales support, the legal department, the weather, the economy, planetary misalignment (I shit you not, "Mars is in Retrograde" was given as a real excuse), and many other reasons for why they somehow aren't responsible for meeting a sales goal requirement.

My usual response (I couldn't and wouldn't respond to astrology excuses) was to clearly define where the issues lay and bring them to a conclusion, define the hang-up, and tell them it's their responsibility to get it resolved (sometimes with my help). You need to clearly state that time is of the essence and this is their job.

Don't get suckered in.

C. "I wasn't trained on that"

If you ever hear the words, "I wasn't trained for/aware of that (insert: product, system, goal/budget)", beware! It could be a trap.

This is dangerous, because you have now been exposed to someone using plausible deniability. Plausible deniability, as it applies to a sales rep, is the act of claiming they have/had no responsibility or knowledge of a task required of them.

Over the years, I have taken on new roles within sales organizations where this type of excuse was rampant (and, even worse, accepted). On occasion, I have discovered that what the rep was saying was true... they really didn't know that this was a part of their role. But usually, no. They're trying to bullshit you into believing that they've been out of the loop.

If you find that this rep is leveraging this as an excuse, it's up to you to call them on their bluff. Train this person on the information or task "needed", then set them on their way. (Please make sure to take notes and document your actions, because when this person quits months later, it *will* come up with HR).

Most of the time, when a salesperson(s) gives you this excuse it's because they have been allowed to get away with it in the past. By you "training" them on it, you are defusing the excuse and alleviating the fictional failure on their part. In time, these personnel will know that the gig is up and leave the company. Hopefully.

I had once taken over a small sales telephone team where there were a mix of some in-house reps and some remote. Prior to me coming on board, the manager over this team was pretty loosey-goosey. He was more interested in being looked up to (having his ass kissed) than actually being an effective manager. Thus, the reason for me being hired.

One of the first things I did was sit down with each of his reps and discuss their sales styles (sales styles will be discussed later), how to best communicate with them, and what they have in the pipeline.

One of the typical questions I asked the first rep:

Me: *"Where are you on your budget?"*

To which the rep responded: "Budget? I don't know…"

Me: "Your budget. Your goal…? Quarterly…? Yearly…?"

The rep: "I don't have a budget, no one has ever asked me that before…"

Me: "What do you mean? What is your monthly sales goal?"

The rep: "I don't know… it's never been discussed…"

I immediately called bullshit. Not having and not knowing a sales goal (weekly, monthly, quarterly, yearly) is unheard of. It just doesn't happen. How does the team – and, more importantly, the CEO - know if they're hitting a corporate goal? I didn't believe them.

Annnnnd… I was wrong. They didn't know because the "VP of Sales" seemed to have been operating without a budget?!?

This is some of the complete madness that you will inherit in your new role.

On another occasion, I asked a company veteran why he hadn't been updating his prospects and dealing with the CRM. He stated, "I was never trained on that…"

With this statement, he had just told me three things:

1) He was full of shit, because the CRM had been in place for 3 years and others were using it daily. On earlier visits to the market, CRM results were covered with the managers and directors who reported into me.
2) The managers were covering for him as he had some of the larger sales accounts in the company.
3) He did not feel he needed to input his information because he was above doing the work - or just lazy.

As it turned out... he and his manager left. I suspect they didn't like the training which followed, including the subsequent changes and responsibilities I had requested. (Side note: After a bit of adjustments to his accounts and redistribution to different reps, his accounts began billing 3x as much from the previous years)

D. Consistently writing fictional prospects or clients

One of the games some reps play is the fictional prospect game. They usually do this because they think you aren't paying attention or won't request to see their prospect list on a consistent basis.

Call their bluff. Ask for a list of prospects and clients each week and compare what was provided week after week. Press them for details on what has transpired, including amounts and estimated times for contract closures.

This might sound like a given task as a sales manager, but you would be shocked to know how often this is not consistently done.

It should also be noted that if you don't flush out the fiction in your team's pipeline, you are opening yourself up to misjudging your pacing to the budget goal. This means you're being told that your reps have $1M in the pipeline to close, but in reality it's less than half of that. Everyone ends up losing in these scenarios.

E. Ghost appointments / ghost calls

When I have a sales team that's struggling or has a big budget gap, I ask to do a ride-alongs with the sales team. I do this not as a punishment, but as a way to access the reasons for the gaps and help try to close sales calls.

As you might expect, the underperforming sales reps also underperform at bringing you along on this type of effort. When pressed on getting some appointments on the books, you begin to see a trend. That trend is appointments that are either no-shows or are just not there. I call these "Ghost Appointments"; where the rep is setting things up to look like they're being constructive.

Again, don't get suckered into the giant time wasters.

F. Trying to beat the system

In the world of cloud-based sales support systems and CRM, reporting has never been more robust and detailed. These reports give you a wonderful fifty-thousand-feet view on the team prospects and future (we'll cover CRMs later), as well as details about what's happening with individual personnel. This can be a great help when you have certain reps that are struggling to meet budgets or goals. It's the perfect way to dive into those platforms and understand why.

Experience has shown me that if you look at the data on the surface, where everything looks great across all of the KPIs, you will start to see that the rep in question has a number of outbound calls which are up to the team standards, that their talk time is up to standard, but their sales are not. Something doesn't make sense...

Well, the devil is in the details. What I suggest you do is dig a little further into these calls - listen to them and what is or isn't being said. Check the numbers that were being dialed and truly understand how your systems define call times (i.e. is the phone system logging from the time that the phone was dialed, or from the moment of pick up on the other side?)

What you will find is that, at times, the rep is trying to play the system and put in trash information and false calls in order to present the illusion that they are doing the work. Basically, they're trying to deceive you and the company.

This happens a lot when you look at teams that are underperforming. At one time I was managing a very large outbound telephone sales team that had individuals whom stated that they were doing all the work, but weren't making the sales. Upon doing a deep review of their calls via information submitted in the CRM, I found that they were calling fax machines and weather update lines to make it look like they were on the phone for longer than they were and/or repeatedly call the same number, over and over throughout the day, in order to boost the total number of outbound calls. This type of thing was rampant and the manager at the time had taken the sales reps for their word that they were doing the right thing. It was a mess.

To resolve this deception, I called all thirty five of the sales reps into the conference room and presented what I had discovered while not revealing who was responsible. I stated that anyone caught manipulating the company records and data from this point moving would be fired on the spot. No questions asked (this was a "Right to Work" state).

The manipulation stopped for a couple of weeks, then started again with a couple of individuals. They were then publicly walked off the sales floor. It wasn't a problem after that.

Check the validity of your team data and information on a regular basis and make sure the team knows you're checking. It's always a good tool to keep everyone on their toes.

Chapter 4

Curve Balls and Traps from Your Founder/ CEO /VPs

Just like your reps, there are bosses (the Founder, CEO, VP, and Director) who may try to throw you off or generally screw you (usually over money). It's important to be able to see these moves coming and avoid them for as long as you can. As mentioned earlier, the average time a sales manager lasts is 19 months. Why? I suspect they feel that we're disposable; that because all the heavy lifting has now been done or everything is running more smoothly, you can be replaced with a cheaper model.

One major caveat before we continue in this section: Unfortunately, I suck at "Managing Up" (or kissing people's asses). What you see is what you get with me. I do the job - and I do it very, very well - but I am all about getting to that goal. I don't talk about the traffic, the weather, or last night's game because I couldn't give two shits. But your CEO might. They might like to chit-chat bullshit about a Netflix series, which I might think is childish, predictable, and something to which I won't have a quick response. I struggle to play along, laugh, and smile.

This - along with my stoic professional style, which is similar to a professional poker player - means I lack outward emotion and can be hard for others to read. Plus my tendency to be overly proactive in doing things without explaining every. single. granular. step. can be annoying for a CEO who wants to know the how and why on everything.

My failure to manage up - and experiences having been burned a number of times in past roles - has created a feeling of distrust at even the best of times. This distrust builds over time when early promises begin to mutate into delayed compensation agreements and/or the failure to award a title. Some (a lot, actually) will fail to give you what you're worth or chastise you over subjective matters that are usually unsubstantiated or not core to your role.

This is true even when you're putting in 50- or 60-hour work weeks and everyone is seeing huge year over year sales results. Even when you're managing two departments. Here are some things to look out for:

- Not increasing your salary year over year

- Changing your compensation plan for less

- Changing your compensation plan a month before it comes to payout

- Not paying your bonus or only paying it partially

- Not offering to change an agreed title by an agreed date

- Undermining you with your direct reports

- Placing blame on you for something that is neither your role nor your department

These all sound bad - and they are. When they happen to you, it's a total shock to the system. Especially when you've poured your heart into the role and your team, only to be shorted on your agreed payment (this is why you're doing the job, after all... for pay). You and your employer should have signed a contract; to not fulfill that contract is a feeling of betrayal.

This feeling only grows when you're given a completely subjective or false narrative as the reason for these professional slights. I've been told that I was making too much money or got lucky hitting this particular budget or goal. Or this person <u>said</u> this or <u>felt</u> that earlier in the year.

Usually these reasons are so unsubstantiated or so gray that it's hard to grasp that what's coming out of their mouths is real. I suspect they don't believe what they're saying is real, but want to flex their power or see if they can pull this bullshit excuse off.

When and if this type of scenario occurs, you can do one of two things:

1) You sign the paper and take it because you need the job. No shame in that. I have beautiful children, I know jobs are hard to find in a down economy, and - like everyone - I have financial responsibilities. Suck it up, live another day...

Or

2) The first thing you should do is pump the brakes on the rest of the conversation. Don't sign anything and try your best to walk out of the conversation as politely as possible. Before you leave, say - very clearly - that you will need to take some time to review and reflect over what was said, as well possibly have someone review this. (If they say you have 24 hours to review and sign, that's bullshit. There's no time frame. If it's pressed by your superior or HR, just state it's in your attorney's hands.)

This will immediately throw a flag up on the play and stop any forward momentum with your superior or your superior's superior. You are basically saying, "I understand that you are trying to screw me and I am going to get an attorney involved."

If you go with option number 2, one of two things are going to happen: 1) You are telling everyone not to fuck with you because you expect to be treated fairly and paid accordingly. 2) You have put a target on your back and it's a matter of time before they (your superior and/or HR) pull the plug on you. Things can then become pretty petty from there, so choose well.

Again, this is a terrible thing that happens regularly in the sales world. It's an unfortunate and traumatizing experience to have to continue to work under.

Chapter 5

Rep Sales Styles

Like every color in the rainbow, reps come in all kinds of different flavors (this is not a typo). I consider everyone an individual, but when it comes to work ethic on the sales floor, you can break down reps into a number of types. Here are just a handful:

1) The Lone-Wolf

Almost every experienced sales team has one of these. This is typically a sales individual that works diligently with little to no supervision (because they wouldn't take your supervision anyway). They come in to work, hit their number, and leave. Usually you wouldn't know that they were even there if you didn't do a one-on-one meeting. These are people you can count on to hit their number and, every once in a while, get a big deal. This, however, is not their strong suit. If you ask for more out of them, prepare for push back.

*Side note: Some of the best Lone Wolfs I have worked with are ex-sales-managers who either burned out from the job, or like the money better on the direct sales side versus being responsible for managing the chaos of upper management and a sales team. They know or have an idea of what's happening without asking or you having to explain it. They will be the first person to push back if there's a compensation structure change. They will fight hard to maintain or increase their list if another rep is to leave. They will not, however, take on more work without being paid for it. Also, their CRM data will usually be just enough to give you an idea of what they're up to and just enough to keep them out of trouble. Again, they know the game... they'll play along.

2) Super Hustler

The Super Hustler is a sales individual who will take any and every deal that can be jammed into the system. They usually have endless amounts of energy and have a smile on their face every single day. There could be a nuclear explosion outside and they'd tell you it's a beautiful day! These people are so damn positive that they're impervious to the negative energy that comes from a disenchanted client or hearing "no" from prospects all day. They are a joy to manage as they invigorate the entire sales floor.

*Side note: These types of sales reps are wonderful - so wonderful that everyone wants to hire them. If your team is out of line on compensation structures, budget requirements, or upper management styles, they're gone. I have watched it time and time again; I've lost these fantastic examples of sales personnel, only to be offered a larger salary and commission because my CEO is unwilling to pay for quality people. And when that CEO or human resources manager begins to see the turnover trend with a couple of these big personnel losses, it's usually too late. The CEO will get pissed and blame you for not keeping this person. This is where the CEO will try to drop in and take over with a Hail Mary, trying to retain this person with a higher salary and title, but the damage is done and we all look stupid.

3) The Tactician

This type of salesperson is similar to the Lone Wolf, just more personable. They're more of an engineer than a salesperson. They can give you finite detail of each account and timeframes specific to when things are going to close. These types of sales reps take a while for their pipeline to build as they are far less likely to deviate outside of their comfort zone. When times get a little tough and if budgets aren't being met, they're good for a little bump in new sales, but it falls outside of their operational pattern.

This type of salesperson is fantastic for products with long sales cycles. They are diligent at chipping away at the prospect and/or client to get to the close.

4) Whale Hunter

Ohhhhhhhhhhh, The Whale Hunter! The one type of sales rep that will give you the full tour of emotions, from sheer pain and annoyance to back-flipping joy.

I can't tell you how many Whale Hunters I've had to put on a Performance Plan, only for them to close two or three massive clients. It's like they only become fully engaged in the sales process when the pressure is on and their back is against the wall.

I've been in meetings with human resources - or the CEO/VP, or both - when they're absolutely ripping into the particular person for not making any or continuous sales. This is usually a likeable person, but they're just not getting the job done. I have to pull them in, walk them through the performance plan, and then two or three weeks later... BOOM! The largest account we've ever closed. I can't explain it. They must need this kind of pressure to perform.

*Side note: The Whale Hunter has other faults. For one, their sales go up and down with long dry spells, which can be maddening. The other is that their account list will be top heavy, meaning that they have two or three huge accounts with no small ones. If one or two of those accounts go away, then they're screwed. You're screwed. Be careful.

5) Two-in-One

I've worked in some companies that let two working moms split their work up and function as one rep. This seemed like an overly complicated scenario in a high-paced sales role, but it actually worked. It worked well. They can actually better handle larger accounts or more complicated clients.

Basically, two hustlers shared accounts, worked those accounts, and double-teamed the prospects and clients to maximize optimal sales results. Each sales rep in this scenario took responsibility for what they excelled at, which could be that one was good at building presentations and entering data into the system, while the other could be better at handling demanding clients. Regardless, they both had the similar goal of making money. Their sales rep scenario worked because one could motivate or bounce an idea off the other. They kept each other sane.

Side note: This type of "Two-in-One" rep scenario won't always work. Both of the reps must have had a positive history or trusting one another, as well as develop a system to evenly distribute the workload...

Another Side Note: This all sounds great - until it doesn't. Meaning that if they begin to slip in meeting the budget, you'll be having to write up two at one time. If one is struggling to pull their weight, it can make for an odd dynamic. That and you can have two gang up on you all at once.

6) Clutch Player

The Clutch Player is similar to a "Closing Pitcher" in baseball; you can rely on them to put the sales numbers up when you need it most. This person has an innate ability to get you and the team as close to (or over!) your monthly or yearly goals as possible. They will do anything to get to that goal.

If I have one or more Clutch Players on my sales team, I usually offer additional bonuses, bounties, or perks to them if they can make a predetermined number. This type of sales rep enjoys the attention of reaching something that the others cannot. These are the same people who will make 200 cold calls a day towards the end of the month, just to get in those additional sales/bonuses.

Side note: This type of sales rep should not be confused with The Hustler, as the Clutch Player can be far messier and likely has a dark side. This sales rep will play in the gray areas of sales, knowing they can bend the rules on pricing, product offerings, and add-ons to get to the number that you and upper management want. This bending of the rules is not illegal, but if you allow it then they will abandon the usual sales protocols. They are opportunists who will wait or sand bag deals until you approach everyone to meet the need of hitting a goal or curing a gap in the budget. They will intentionally wait so they can get a bit more of a bonus or perk dollars for those additional sales.

If you have a Clutch Player, you need to keep both an eye and tight rein on them. If you're not watching closely, they will try to squeeze in a deal or two that's borderline unfeasible or not doable at all. If you don't keep close tabs on this rep, they can cause irreparable damage to the sales organization.

I've adopted or acquired teams that had no control over their Clutch Players. They had written up contracts that others had turned a blind eye to; when those contracts failed to pay or were expecting more... well, it was the company that was left holding the bag.

7) The Sponge

The Sponge is the just that - a sponge on the entire team and its resources. This is a rep that consistently fails to make cold calls and/or relies on others to generate opportunities for them. This type of rep will buddy up to anyone within the company that can feed them back channel customer care calls or business requests. This is a rep who convinces your sales development reps (or SDRs) to send them calls.

This is the same person who has survived long enough to acquire an account list, since so many other reps have left.

Side note: These reps are true pieces of work. They're very comfortable taking on another person's labor and calling it their own, not to mention taking the commission along with it. Your sales team will usually have a low opinion of this person's abilities.

8) Blind Chicken

"Even a blind chicken can get to the grain every once in a while…"

The Blind Chicken is the sales rep that's struggling to make any sales, even with all the attention and training you can offer. Every now and then, the Blind Chicken will make a sale and everyone will cheer. Maybe this will be a breakthrough moment and they'll begin to hit their stride… But sooner or later, they fall back into their non-selling ways.

Unfortunately, this poor rep won't be around long.

Chapter 6

The Poisoned Well Syndrome

While we're talking about curveballs that reps can throw, there's also something I call "The Poisoned Well Syndrome". This is when or where there's a dark feeling looming over the sales team. It's not something that's seen on the surface, but has to be observed with both eyes open and without bias.

"A Poisoned Well" is when a certain salesperson or persons are negatively impacting the overall health of the team. This is caused when someone's words or actions directly affect the day-to-day perspective of the team in a negative manner.

You can have a team that's performing well, not great, and you know they're capable of doing more. But they just aren't and you can't figure out why. It's probably because one person or person is dragging down the others.

It's a fact that within any sales organization, you have strong outgoing personalities (that's the reason you hired them) with strong voices and/or opinions. Because of this, you can have a couple of stand-out personalities that can take on the alpha role when you're not around. This can and will become a problem if not corrected.

A prime example of this is when you have a strong personality chastising or bullying other reps in a direct or passive manner. This will certainly occur in a group sales pit environment or in group chats where one or two parties are taking the brunt of the majority of the jokes. Typically, the more that pressure is put on the team, the more the bullying occurs. Then it becomes a regular thing where everyone piles on the target or they begin to take pop-shots at anything that moves on the floor. The majority of this commentary is to get a laugh out of the team and break up the monotony, but the laugh comes at someone else's expense. I believe that sales reps should have some level of thick skin, but if the passive aggressive poking and prodding isn't addressed, it can become a cancer that spreads negativity and dread throughout the organization.

Inversely, if you have a consistent underperformer with a constant need for attention, this can have a similar effect. It's like a classroom teacher who can't get through their lesson because they are having to constantly address the child with outbursts; it will have an overall bad effect on the rest of the room's ability to achieve.

Luckily, the latter (the underperformer) are easier to put on a performance plan where they will either straighten out or crash and burn. The bullying individual or group that's picking on each other can be far more difficult.

As mentioned earlier, you really have to pay attention to what's happening; this type of behavior can and usually will come from your top performing reps. Top performing reps that have big egos, that can smell fear, and gravitate to punishing others in order to prop up that ego.

This is where it can become tricky, based on the salesperson's personality traits, to determine if and when you address your concerns to the bully. You have to have specific examples that are quantifiable and can be backed up. Again, since this is human resources territory, you can't offer opinions that can be interpreted as subjective; then you could be seen as a bully. Yep, they could flip the script on you!

Because you're going up against strong personalities, make sure you have all of your facts and are ready to blow back. If you have a true "Poison Well" scenario and have, in fact, found the person or persons who are responsible, there's a very good chance that they will be very vocal with the rest of the sales team - and anyone else. Let them.

Let them get everything stirred up. They will openly begin to "Poison" the sales environment and may even try to engage you. This can be testing you with disingenuous questions in sales meetings, purposely underperforming, trying to circumvent your authority and protocols, or - even crazier (depending on how persuasive they are with the team) - encouraging passive mutinies such as getting everyone to consistently leave early for drinks.

You just never know what one or two of these people are willing to do. Not only do you have to be patient, but your upper management and human resources also need to be patient and trust you. However, over time these people will screw up because they just can't help it. And when they do, step in and correct it. Do it both in the open and then in a one-on-one with human resources.

This process can take days, weeks, or months. But I can guarantee you, once you pluck the bad actor from your team, the negative fog will lift and your team will begin to excel.

Chapter 7

Hiring a Sales Team / Human Resources

For whatever reason, I always get asked the same question(s) when I'm consulting or considering working with a new company; "What do you look for in a new sales hire?" or "How do you deal with an underperforming sales rep?"

This means one of two things: either they want you to let someone go as soon as you come onboard, or there's a lingering issue that you will need to address because they're uncomfortable or inexperienced. Basically, they aren't good at letting people go. Which is a part of the job.

What's really interesting about this hiring and firing is that the majority of the time, human resources cannot be found - or they delegate this responsibility to you by saying; "Well you understand who you want to hire, so maybe you should handle it..." or "They're your rep. It's probably better that you do all the talking. I'll sit and offer support." I really struggle to understand what value the HR department head brings outside of processing state and federal paperwork. Oh, buying cakes for employees' birthdays.

On Hiring Sales Personnel

This may sound kind of corny, but when hiring someone for a sales role, I'm looking for some kind of light in their eyes. Plus a level of confidence and conviction to sell themselves to you.

Stage 1: Review the Resume

You can't really tell much about a person's personality or how convincing they are by looking at their resume. I usually look for timeframes at earlier positions, gaps in employment, spelling errors, and education. I'm looking to avoid jumpers and/or scammers who will have amazingly unrealistic roles, responsibilities, and accomplishments. It's not that those people can't have great accomplishments, it's just that if they have them then they're applying for the wrong job. If they look well rounded and everything matches up, I go to stage 2.

Stage 2: The Screener Call

The screener call is essential first contact with a possible candidate. It basically sets the stage for the next steps in your process. On these screener calls (which last no more than 10 minutes), I briefly introduce myself, my role, and my time with the company. I then discuss the company and the role for which we are hiring. I'm typically upfront with the rep on the compensation and expectations of the role so we don't waste each other's time.

Next I ask the candidate questions about their current and previous roles and experience, as well as how those align with our role. As they are speaking, I am listening to how they sound over the phone. Are they clear and concise? How is their pronunciation and vocabulary? What is the tone - are they bright and peppy or nervous? Do they use humor? Are they pulling me in with subject manner to have a longer conversation? And, more importantly, have they done their research around the company and the role?

Within 5 minutes I know whether this person is going to qualify. If they have me engaged for 10 minutes, I request a face-to-face meeting.

Stage 3: The Face-to-Face

Now, if you're in a role where you are responsible for hiring employees, this might not be news to you, but there's an epidemic in recruiting called "Ghosting".

Ghosting is when you agree to meet with a candidate at a certain day and time for an interview, but they just don't show up... No calls to say something came up, no email thanking you for the opportunity but saying they've taken another role... nothing. They just don't show up. Because the "Ghosting" epidemic is so prevalent, you have to screen and book three times more candidates than usual to get a solid return on your time.

If and when candidates do show up, I usually jump right in and start going into great detail about the company and role information that was and was not covered in the earlier screening. During the interview I am listening to their questions, watching if they are taking notes, and looking to see if they are paying attention. When I ask them questions, are they looking me in the eye? Are they confident in their responses? In the back of my mind, I'm thinking of the role they will be filling and whether their personality matches the team. I think "Is this person trainable?"

Tell-tale signs that this is not the right person for the role is someone who looks like they just rolled out of bed after a three-day drunken bender (this has happened to me a number of times and will happen to you). Is their clothing ironed and put together in a professional manner? Basically, if they look like they don't give a shit, then this is a mistake. You can typically cut those loose.

Within a 45-minute to hour-long conversation with a candidate, I know if I want to move forward. From there I have maybe one other manager lean in and ask a round of questions to get their insight and make sure I'm not missing something or being overly biased.

Then I start the process of drafting the offer and required paperwork. I usually don't ask for referrals because if the candidate had any sense at all he or she would give a list of people to sing their praises, so it's a total waste of time.

The real fact of the matter is if this person has all the abilities to be a great salesperson, they will. If they don't, they won't. If they're underperforming, you take the step to address that underperformance.

Addressing Underperformance

I guess when someone thinks of the sales manager or director role, they truly don't understand the breadth of training, motivation speaking, and driving activity. I truly believe that they discount the role, especially when the sales manager is making it look easy.

But it's not easy… far from it, in fact. When you have a sales rep that's underperforming, your number of tasks (and stress) double. Because now you're having to micromanage someone to generate a preferred outcome. Getting to that preferred outcome can become a painful process for all parties. Here are the steps I've used to manage an underperforming representative(s).

Recognizing the Gaps in Performance

If and when you have a rep that's underperforming, you clearly have to understand where and why that underperformance is happening. Is it the number of calls, number of prospects, struggling with a type of decision maker, handling objections, not being firm enough, unable to get past a gatekeeper…? Those can all be trained and fixed.

The real problems accrue when the rep is just not doing the work and is giving unsubstantiated reasons, "No one is picking up the phones…" and "So-and-so is taking my accounts…" or "I have a bad territory/region…" and, of course, "Everyone is not closing or canceling because <u>blank</u> (add in sales support, billing, legal) isn't doing their job…" (*Please note, the excuses listed can be real. They really could have crappy territory and the legal department may be sitting on a contract that's going to blow the deal(s), but those are your problems to solve, not theirs.)

You should also make sure that there aren't any real issues in your products, pricing, and go to market strategies that may be influencing why this rep and others are underperforming (see section on "Not making budget").

But if there truly is a scenario where the rep isn't doing the work, you have to set stage to cure the underperformance. The steps are simple:

Step 1: Seeing a Trend

Address that you are seeing a trend in possible underperformance. This, again, can be: Not enough calls, not enough prospects being added to the funnel, not enough demos, not enough contracts being sent out, and, of course, not enough closes.

I have this conversation with every rep. I have these conversations with even the high performing reps. Sometimes I could be misinterpreting the information or just want to stir it up by having them fight back (poke the bear - clearly show who is in charge).

When I address these trends and there is a reason to be concerned, I lightly state that if I don't see an uptick in results within a certain amount of time (usually two weeks), we will be forced to build out a plan. The PIP, aka the infamous Performance Improvement Plan… Dah, dah-dahhhhh! (sounds of doom).

Step 2: The Performance Plan

There are plenty of templates and instructions out there on how to construct a performance plan for your failing rep (just Google it). However, you need to make sure that whatever you plan to put in front of the rep has the blessing (via email confirmation) of the human resources department. This is because, if your rep wants to contest the document or you, it must be able to stand as an airtight document in court. It is or can be used as a basic legal document. Once fully discussed and clearly understood by all parties, three copies (one for you, one for HR, and one for them) need to be signed by the rep.

The substance of the Performance Improvement Plan should be structured around very specific requested tasks and a defined timeframe. If those tasks are not completed by that time, the rep will be let go. The time frame varies based on the situation. If you have a short sales cycle of 2-3 weeks, you can set the time frame to be tighter. For longer sales cycles of 2-6 months, you will have to offer a full business quarter to see quantifiable results.

Requested tasks vary based on your company's business verticals, sales protocols, and processes, but all eventually fall into the same requests: hit a total number of KPIs, get calls, demos, contracts out, and hit a specific budget as requested. Because I want the rep to succeed, I ask for them to add me to a total number of calls and/or presentations per week. Not as a punishment, but to help evaluate where I can help, such as closing deals or shoring up their pitch language.

As you begin and continue to note your rep's results through the performance plan process, there should be no tasks that are collected and recorded that are subjective and non-quantifiable. This means they cannot share a perceived opinion that is not supportable and/or not fact based. You have to remove your feelings from the results of the reps.

* Please note that there is no specific timeline when executing these stages. Some reps fall in and out of sale role requirements all the time. Sometimes it might take up to year or more to justify to both parties that the role is not a good match.

** It should also be noted that the performance plans are designed to help reps overcome and straighten up their performances. These are not documents to harass or cajole employees who you dislike or want to remove from your department. If that is your intent, then you are a bad manager who likely doesn't know how to hire or manage. I have watched managers execute PIPs like the postal service delivers mail. It becomes a shitty sales environment. The reps don't trust the manager and it creates discontent amongst the fellow employees who then begin to look for an exit plan. Basically, it sets the stage for the belief that there's no future with this department or company. They all know it's just a matter of time before it's one of them.

Firing

If the rep in question has fulfilled the required tasks (and, more importantly, hit their budget), you and the rep feel great! Both of you should come out of the performance plan timeline with a stronger professional bond and a clear understanding of each other's strengths and weaknesses as professionals.

If the rep begins to fail through the Performance Improvement Plan, you need to start drafting the employee termination document to let the rep go. Again, this document and it's procedures should be okayed and/or supplied by the human resources department. When drafting the document, you need to clearly illustrate all the agreed details of the performance plan and the results - or lack thereof - agreed upon at the meeting. Again, there should be no opinion or tones shared... just the facts. Have human resources personnel review and okay the document before presentation.

Define with your human resources department when this document will be shared with the rep and require that they are present. Never present one of the documents without a witness in the room or on the phone.

Once everyone is there, read through the document, have human resources answer any questions, and walk the rep to the door. That's it.

While this might sound cold, it really isn't. If you've worked with the rep to try to achieve what needs to be done in the performance plan, then you know whether their head is in it to hit the goals requested. If they resist you and fight every aspect of the plan, you know pretty quickly that it's not going to work. Usually the rep flames out (or lashes out) for not being accountable for detailed tasks. Thankfully, this typically happens within the first few weeks. When you do set them down to let them go, they are usually expecting it and there should be no surprises.

Letting someone go sucks, but you have to get used to it. You're being paid to generate results, not running an island of broken toys.

Immediately relay to your team that this person was let go and tell them that it is not a reflection of them, as they are meeting the goals of the team. You shouldn't relay specifics of why or what transpired during the process. It's none of their business and, if any of that information was relayed, you can put yourself and the company into legal uncertainties if the rep should say they were let go for unsubstantiated reasons.

Be honest with them, then get back to work.

Chapter 8

Clearly Defining a "Lead", from a "Suspect" to a "Prospect"

One of the greatest gray areas in handling sales reps (especially new ones) is getting them to understand a true "sales prospect". Where your job comes into play is to clearly define a "lead", a "suspect", and a "sales prospect".

If you don't address, clarify, and reinforce each of these terms early, your CRM sales pipeline will be chock-full of bullshit fiction and wishful thinking. I've taken on new sales manager roles where reps will list every contact they made on the street, in the neighborhood, and on the bus ride home as possible prospects. I don't believe that your reps do this on purpose; it's usually that they have been missed by the manager (the reason you are there), trained, or held to any consistent standard.

Another reason there is so much confusion around how and why we define these key elements that direct effect our day-to-day sales lives is that our CRMs call them something different. With each CRM there's a new name. I suspect they do this because they want to stay out of some litigation over intellectual property laws between them and the other thousand CRMs out there, but regardless. As the CRMs attorneys try to evade the courtrooms, their marketing teams come up with new wiz-bang names for each element. They might title or create a section where leads live in a "Working" or where suspects live in a "Following". This all nonsensical tech gibberish that the CRM companies use to sell their products wares. If you can't go into that CRM and change those names, it will confuse the shit out of everyone.

*Side note: While we're talking about making changes to a CRM before you roll it out to your team. Please, I beg with you... I plead to you... please, please, please... take all the non-essential steps out of the team's CRM workspace. They don't need to see and I don't need to see every stinking designation or made-up bullshit KPI offered in there, like "Emailed", "Emailed back", "Scheduled Demo", "Attempted Follow-up", "Pre-Negotiation", "Discussed our dogs", and "Wore the same color shirt"... This is all a complete blur of nonsense and creates noise over what truly needs to be done. Please stop. It also creates a sales culture of people who can bullshit the best. There's already enough in your day-to-day, so try not to make it worse. If the marketing team or CEO requests you add the crazy designations, tell them no. "Sorry, no." Explain why.

What is a Lead?

A "lead" is a piece of data with contact information like name, phone number (business or personal), email, title, and/or address. This lead data should be specific to the business industry that you and your team are currently or planning on targeting for sales.

It should be noted that this is just data. This data that could be erroneous, faulty, or out of date. It could have been collected by someone or some party under nefarious circumstances (data scraping software) or false pretenses. Either way, it's just a name and numbers until that data has been contacted and clarified.

What is a Suspect?

A suspect is when the lead data has been contacted and you and your team have confirmed that the data is, in fact, correct and they match the industry being targeted.

Depending on your sales and marketing teams' capabilities and contact strategies, once the data is confirmed your team can begin adding this suspect's information into the CRM. That means they can be remarketed to with additional brand, promotions, and public relations materials.

What is a Prospect?

Only when the suspect has been presented to and has **_confirmed,_** via an email or verbally, that they want to move forward in the sales process does the suspect become a prospect.

From there, the sales team can and should put the prospect under sales opportunity.

That's it. There's no magic to it.

On CRMs

Before we start in this section, I want to touch off on CRMs. As much as I love customer relation management (CRM) programs and all their organizational abilities, it's important to state that they don't do the job at hand; managing personal and motivating them while generating/ and closing sales.

Working with a group of individuals, day-in and day-out, and driving them to do something consistently challenging like sales cannot be done via colorful charts and wiz-bang integrations with marketing mails. Sales and sales management is a physically and psychologically trying profession which is extremely hard to quantify. Thus, logging calls or notes of prospect conversation is only a small portion of the job.

I completely understand why corporations are in love with CRM technology. It gives the perceived ability of a future outlook and/or control. It also offers the ability to manage information about the client and prospect versus the rep leaving and taking the clients with them.

Typically, when I see over-the-top energy from a CEO/Founder that's applying a CRM as the be-all-end-all sales solution I know it means two things: 1) They don't know shit about sales. 2) They've been sold on the idea that a program is going to

I also completely understand why the reps put total bullshit information into the CRM system. You're basically asking wild extroverts or mental spastics to plot detailed and grainual information in a complex computer system. That's like asking a squirrel to land a fighter jet. It just ain't gonna happen.

If (and only if) information is imputed correctly, a CRM manages sales forecasting, gap analysis, customer outreach, etc.... But what it doesn't do is help nurture your team to be better professionals or, more importantly, close deals. (To be clear, I believe that CRMs are made for middle managers who want to place blame on others while defending their role. There, I said it.)

Truth be told, you should take responsibility for making sure that only specific details are being collected by sales reps. You should focus on making sure it is inputted in a super easy fashion so they will do it often and with the least amount of prospect fiction writing involved. This way, the CRM program is used and can be used for the intended purposes.

I have found a CRM is best utilized by all when all prospects are simply logged in and their contact information is updated. That's it. The CRM should give reminders for follow-ups and where they last left the conversation.

Asking the rep to put in imaginary numbers of where the customer's projected spending levels are going to fall means you get just that: projections. Asking the rep to add the date of when the contract will close is crystal ball reading. The client determines that. When they are ready to make a decision or have the budget available, they will close. Pushing a rep and a client to give that information (unless readily given by the client) is unrealistic and childish. When I have come in to companies that are basically asking their reps for these lengthy financial input requests, the deeper the bullshit gets.

Adding in templated emails responses via the CRM's automation is inauthentic and the best way to ruin a current or future business relationship.

*Look, I get it. These CRM companies have to set themselves apart from the hundred other competitors, meaning they have to continue to be innovative and relevant. But 50% of the tools and capabilities of those CRMs are either not being used or irrelevant to daily use. I also understand that when these CRMs are being sold to upper management, their eyes light up with giddy joy because they believe it will solve all of the issues when it comes to presenting future sales to the shareholders. They don't know or understand the program, nor how much labor it takes to make it work... They just like the possibilities. They were sold on it. It then becomes your problem to make it happen.

Part 2

The Crescendo Pitch Strategy

Like with every great piece of creative work, be it a song, movie, or speech, there is a certain flow or pattern that establishes it as worthy of supporting, listening to, or watching.

This section covers how to structure your approach and dialogue while presenting. It is a concept of knowing where you are in the presentation, how to keep yourself from getting off track, and how to convey a succinct and convincing message. Crescendo Sales can be applied to a simple or complex presentation with short or long timeframes. As long as you understand its parts and pieces, it can be adopted or modified for any situation.

Over a determined timeframe, these pieces lead to a peak of high energy or a triumphant end. A crescendo. Thus, the name for the strategy.

The Crescendo Sales Strategy relies on preparation, self-awareness, and listening to the responses of the parties receiving the presentation. I won't be covering gimmick tactic approaches that try to manipulate the receiving parties into a push/pull volley of questioning. These approaches sell lots of books, fit into only a handful of situations, are quickly forgotten, and disintegrate when the parties realize they are being manipulated.

This is about controlling how you take ownership of the presentation timeframe while being conscientious of the receiving party's time.

The Crescendo Sale Strategy is broken down over 7 stages:

1) Research and Preparation
2) The Opening
3) Level Setting
4) The "Current State"
5) The Solution(s)
6) The Resolution
7) The Finish

Stage 1: Research and Preparation

Before I even pick up the phone to begin a cold call or walk into a prospect's business, I do a bit of research. Now this might seem like a pretty obvious first step in the sales process, but you might also be shocked at how little (or none) is done prior to making first contact. By not doing the research, you're basically saying I don't give a shit, I'll fly blind, and I'll pray that I get lucky. 95% of the time, you will fail to close any prospect or business with this strategy.

I mean, how else are you going to have a business conversation? The prospect is busy and usually doesn't want to be bothered. You need to be able to break through the noise that's happening at that moment in the prospect's mind and environment. You can do that by discussing the damn weather and last night's big plans. They couldn't give a shit. They could be handling a small emergency and you're in the way.

I could almost guarantee you that if you walk in with nothing, you will walk out with nothing. You should strive to have quality conversations, not to embarrass yourself and your company. Your closing percentages will go up just because you have the confidence and the talking points to have a constructive conversation.

Questions you need to know, at the very least, before walking in:

- Who is the primary decision maker? (Title/ Time with Company / Experience)

Sorry, but this is a no-brainer. You need to know who you're trying to get in touch with. What's their role? Do they have the power to make a financially binding decision within a company?

Too many times I have been on what the rep has determined a "closing call", only to find out that the prospect is a middle manager with no authority to make decisions. Basically, we had wasted everyone's time and had to start all over again. It's usually not a complete loss, thankfully, because the prospect is fully vetted with our product by then and can be the internal flag bearer within the targeted company.

- What is the core product and service?

Different decision makers can have different responsibilities and products within a large company. What you might believe to be the core product or service of that company might not be what you think it is, or there could be sub-products that aren't openly present.

It's your job to find out what this is.

- The target consumer audience?

In a similar fashion to core products and services, you need to clearly define and understand the prospective company's consumer or target audience. Is there a specific size company they are trying to target? Services? Etc.

Again, you might think you know or have an idea of who their target audience is, but you could be totally off. Just ask. The worst thing that could happen is you assume you know the target, build a presentation addressing this target, and find out you were wrong. That equals a disaster.

- What's the market size? Market penetration?

It's important to at least know the prospect's market size (or Universe) before going in. Assuming that a prospect's market size only serves a certain state or region could be leaving money on the table and / or rub the prospective contact the wrong way. They could perceive you and your company as a small player.

For instance, you speak to prospects that you know only under a local business and present, only to then find out that they are part of a global corporate entity. Your pitch to this prospect has now tripled in scale.

- Average product or service ticket price? Current sales?

Knowing the average ticket price per product and/or service helps you to understand how your product or solution can amplify this prospect's opportunities. It's the brass tacks of what's at stake - it's why we're all here...

If you can pull data on where the prospect was for sales last year, as well as a projection of where they're headed in this current year, you will be speaking the prospects language.

- Who are the competitors? What are their benefits?

Pretty basic here. You have to know who the competitors are in the space, then you need to know each player's strengths and weaknesses. Prices, each product's pros and cons, recent changes in company direction, etc. etc.

- What products similar to your services are they currently using?

Having a grasp of what products they are currently using (or not) is mission-critical for crafting your conversation.

Stage 2: The Opening. Warm up the crowd...

You've seen it before - a late night talk show host stands in front of the crowd at the beginning of the show and rattles off current events and topics while curbing their humor or joke. This is called the "Warm up the Crowd "; it allows everyone to settle in for your presentation.

The opening is your typical "small talk" scenario where all parties are settling into their seats, tapping out a final email, and grabbing their refreshment prior to you going into your presentation.

Let's not fool ourselves; this time is a part of the presentation. This is where you see the receiving party's state of mind before you start presenting. What you observe during this time should be recognized and tailored. For instance, if your receiving parties are looking pensive or agitated by something prior to your arrival, you need to be aware of that. You will need to address it before going into the presentation. If they're off somewhere else pondering a problem, there's a strong possibility that your entire performance and presentation will be lost on them. I'm not saying abandon the timeframe with the receiving parties, but it may be a possibility if it isn't self-correct and impossible to overcome.

Many times I have recognized a challenging opening and respectfully said, "Is this a good time? Should we come back a little later?" Typically, this lets the receiving parties know that you have recognized their state of mind. They will hopefully respect your attention to the situation and time, allowing you to move forward or re-schedule for a later time.

The mood going into the opening is paramount to how the rest of the meeting transpires moving forward. I've been in sales pitches in the Mid-West where these last two thirds of the meeting (they're just super nice there). Chit-chatting about the location, sports teams, competitors, and general gossip. I was sitting in, riding shotgun and overseeing the presentation - therefore not running the show - so it seemed to last forever. The sales executive did his short-but-sweet presentation in less than 10 minutes. The client liked it and, before you knew it, we were done. 45 minutes of opening and 10 minutes of presentation. It happens.

The inverse of this is the opening is skipped completely because the receiving party (the prospect/client) wants you to skip the bullshit and just get on with it. That would be what we call a "Cold Opening", where your confidence in your abilities needs to overcome the sometimes cold, quiet, almost sterile environment... Just the empty stare of the client.

This cold opening can go one of three ways.

1) The client isn't interested and is just being polite or finding a way to burn up time during a slow day. This is a terrible situation because you're basically dancing monkeys as they stare blankly with glazed ham eyes... through you... waiting 'til lunch.

2) This prospect/ client has no time or bandwidth to be polite and listen to personal effects. They need to tell you that it's time to hit the gas, get down to business, and hit the high notes (think a Casting Call

situation). Make the most of the situation and be impactful.

3) The last cold opening could be that the client/prospect has no game face, so to show neutral interest, it's better for them to have a flat non-signal approach. This is fine. They'll show all their cards if your performance is exciting and done completely.

Sometimes I can struggle with the opening because I don't really know this person that I'm pitching to. Sometimes you can't pick up any cues from the prospect/client's office or are meeting in a neutral, sterile location like a boardroom. In these cases, when it's important to warm up a room, I'll usually drop back and work a FORD technique: Family, Occupation, Recreation, and Dreams... (yeah, maybe not Dreams...). People LOVE to talk about themselves, so let them do it. The more they talk, the better your bond with them, and the more easily the walls come down.

If I can laugh with the prospect/client before we get started, that's a plus too.

*Side note: Your state of mind

This section should be reflected in the fashion of an actor or director in a play or movie whose script is devised by them. It's your one-(wo)man-show.
As a salesperson (or in HR terminology, individual contributor), you are the actor executing a

predetermined script of your own design. There will be improvisation initiated by the prospect or client (let's not get hung up on that...), which is expected in a theater/movie environment. You feed off the environment, play to that environment, or expand on that environment.

Remember this: If you have dedicated time with the prospect/client, they are looking for a small performance.... Give it to them. It's your responsibility as a professional.

As sales management (in HR terminology, player/coach. I say cat-herder), you are the director. You are responsible for all the parts and pieces of the team and organization achieving a goal every day, month, quarter, and year...

Stage 3: Level Setting. Bring everyone up to speed...

Level setting is the act of accomplishing two things:

1. Establish the credibility of yourself and what/why you're presenting.
2. Establish and recognize to whom you are presenting.

Part one of level setting is taking your time to explain your background, experience, education, etc. It's also a time where you explain commonalities with the receiving parties. This should be shared in a personalized, frank manner; it's not the time to gloat and beat your chest. This allows everyone in the room to understand who you are, why you're there, and the seriousness of what's being presented. You are basically saying "The chit chat has ended, let's get to the business at hand."

(Sidenote: Part one should not be confused with the "Elevator Speech" (a term I detest), which it is not. "Elevator Speech(es)" are reserved for sales hacks reading off of laminated cards. A minute-long "Elevator Speech" begins and ends with the presenter, establishing zero dialogue after it has been spoken.)

Part two allows the receiving parties to explain their backgrounds and speak about their accomplishments. Part two allows them to gain a bit of levity, as well as establish who will be making the decisions or deserves the most attention.

Within any story exists a portion where the characters establish themselves. Sometimes it's just portions of themselves.

"What you told us"

This section of your presentation is fairly basic. Deliver exactly what the receiving parties told you. More specifically, which of their goals, needs, hurdles, and expectations are you planning on addressing and solving?

The main thing that you want to accomplish is have all parties (which includes yourself) on the same page of what is being discussed. While this section might seem like a nuisance and a bit patronizing to the receiving parties, it confirms what's going to be covered and makes sure that there's no issue that's been missed or something that has accrued prior to the presentation.

Stage 4: The "Current State". Establishing the antagonist (the complications)

In the current state, we are discussing and breaking down what they are currently doing and what's happening within the company. The good, the bad, and the ugly. It's a transparent, black and white type of conversation. If there are numbers to present, goals to set, and competitors to analyze, this is the place to do it.

Think of it as presenting your case to the jury. Clearly state all the findings of your research and the conversations you've had up to this point. It's important to show both the good and the bad of what they're doing or have accomplished. Be fair and non-subjective in your delivery of this information.

The better you do your homework and present the prospect information, the more confidence they will have in you. This is building trust. Trust in you, the company, and the product. Don't be shocked to have the prospect(s) chiming in during the presentation, backing your information up and adding additional color to a subject or problem which is not fully flushed out in your data. When they are openly interjecting in the presentation, that means they're following along to where you're taking them. This is good; you're setting yourself up for the next section.

Stage 5: The Solution(s). The TA-DA!

If you've done your homework and presented the facts at hand, you should have been able to put all the puzzle pieces together. Your company's product(s) and solution(s) are the last piece.

If done correctly, when you present your product/service you will have shown how each problem is being solved, how goal(s) are being met, how time and/or money is being saved, and a projected return on investment.

Usually, I and in timelines of how long a process will take transition to launch, budgets / billing is to be released, or when / where the product will gain traction.

When you are in this section of your pitch, you need to think about what questions or objections will be asked. Preemptively, somewhere in your presentation you need to address this with a clear answer(s). It's covering your bases.

If you've gotten this far into the presentation and you get an unanticipated curveball question or objection thrown at you that you can't answer, address it with "I don't know. Let me check with *so-and-so* and get that answer for you..." Then keep moving. Don't let it throw you off.

Side note: If you're pitching to a prospect that was at one time a seasoned sales professional (or still is...), don't be alarmed if they try to throw you off by getting loud, asking nonsensical questions, or just acting uninterested. They're throwing false flags at you. Testing you. They might even try to get you to jump ahead of the presentation to get to the money portion earlier, so they pick you apart over pricing or pieces of the product that might not work. They want to get you out of the groove and test whether your conviction and confidence is real. They want to see if you'll fold under the pressure.

This might be a terrible example, but I used to sell solutions to high-end injury attorneys (the ones with custom suits and exotic cars). Trained debaters in the highest form who make a living engaging in conflict scenarios. Their profession is constantly being approached by salespeople who they expect to try to waste their precious time. They rejected most if not all incoming offers. It wasn't uncommon for them to try to blast me with an avalanche of opinions and objections before I could even get a word out. Things like how they get a call about this type of thing twice a day, how my product is inferior to this or that, how he is too busy to use a product at the moment... etc.

This is how they work - it's their job. Mostly it's the shock and awe tactic. You've got to remember that they fight for a living and wouldn't respect you if you didn't stand your ground. It basically translates to "if you're willing to fold this early in the game, your product would definitely fold just as quick."

Stage 6: The Resolution

Again, if you've followed the steps of the strategy, the resolution is where you have brought everything together, presented the solution, and answered all the questions.

If price or cost details haven't been covered, then this is where it needs to happen.

This is when I ask "If you don't have any other questions... let me give you the elements I need signed to get you started." I then rifle through my things and slide the contracts across the table and act as I start to pack my things. Basically stating, I am done.

Stage 7: The Finish

When posing the assumptive closing question, I am putting them on the spot and evoking one of two things. 1) They say yes and they sign the contract.

Which happens. 2) They start asking more granular questions pertaining to launch timelines, training, license and payment options, and - more importantly - they can get a deal.

On Humor

I am super guilty of running close to the edge with prospects/clients when it comes to humor. To further define that, I mean I get rolling making the client laugh. However, you have to be conscious of letting that high point down easily, because we're going to be covering business topics that sometimes won't be funny. Plus there's another emotional peak that you're trying to reach in your presentation and you don't want it to eclipse.

You don't want to get into a situation where the prospect/client goes, "Jesus, that guy/gal was funny...but I can't remember a damn thing we covered..." Remember we are trying to have a the

Let's Talk About What You're Selling:

The products you are selling can and will affect your ability to perform. It's going to affect your 'Ta-da!' moment. The product - be it a physical and tangible product, a service, or a belief - it needs to have a solution that you truly believe in. Otherwise you won't be able to carry a convincing performance.

I've sold passionless products and services... It can be a grind. It was a constant task to keep myself motivated to sell repetitively.

I've sold products that are so bland (like drill bits... like the ones that drill holes...) that, to me, was about as exciting as watching mold growing. I had to dig to find something that got me excited about drill holes. It turned out that engineers get excited (as much as an engineer can) about holes. Their mild excitement and my lack of excitement translated to marginal sales results.

This lack of excitement can also be affected by poorly managed companies, difficult managers, or clients that just want to be difficult pain in the asses... These can be absolute soul vacuums that make life as a sales professional a pitiful existence. Being a sales professional already has it's emotional peaks and valleys thrown in by a shitty boss, so it can get rough... That's not only another book, but probably not a good use of my time to write - or yours to read.

Don't Ride Shotgun

Typically, I'm okay with others from my company or office sitting in on the presentation. It's fine, as long as they aren't a dead anchor being dragged through the meeting. More importantly, an impediment to your presentation.

I've been in presentations where my accompaniments will not stop talking (talk, talk, talk, talk... rattle on like a pebble in a tin can). They speak out of anxiety over the situation or they feel the need to jump ahead in the material and speed up the presentation - or slow it down.

Sometimes you'll have a person sitting stone-faced and terrified of what's going to come out of your mouth (True story: I've seen this same person covering their face when it comes to the point of discussing money). Or this person will blurt out something to try to beat you to the punch.

If you feel this is going to happen, do one of two things:

1) Ask them not to attend
2) Set some very specific rules of engagement

- Say hello and introduce yourself
- Get comfortable and follow along
- If spoken to, answer shortly and concisely
- Get me a coffee (just kidding... well, maybe... we'll see...)

Note: I'm not saying that the presentation team(s) don't work. I'm just saying that you have to have the confidence in this other person. A person who's going to blow your whole presentation because they're an incompetent, babbling fool in the wrong industry and lacking in any mastery of their profession.

Story Time: Cringe-Worthy Shotgun Rider

Charlotte, NC; Large Law Firm

While managing a sales team in the southern part of the United States, I had the opportunity to pitch a very large and very profitable injury litigation law firm. I have been in many law practices up and down the Eastern seaboard, but this was by far the most impressive (they actually had built a courtroom in the practice... for practice...)

A "seasoned" account executive who was assigned to this particular client, Jerry, had been asked a number of times to set this meeting but had struggled to get it. With a little bit of prodding, Jerry got us 30 minutes with the client. From the moment we broke the seal on the door, I knew that this account executive was going to have an issue. The issue was he had no game plan for any type of presentation and had hoped to bullshit his way into a conversation (this was sad, considering this was what the market considered a seasoned rep).

Within the first three minutes of the rep's babbling, I had to cut him off and reset the meeting (as tactfully as possible). I went into my presentation (I had a game plan) and led the client to the solution that matched the firm's current needs. As I got to portion on cost, I looked over at the account rep who literally had his hands covering his face while slumped over. He was scared of the number that was going to come out of my mouth... "$20,000... per month". The client did not balk or buck. He said, "Okay... I'll need to move some things in the budget... What else?..."

The law firm bought the program eventually... and unfortunately Jerry left soon after... It's unfortunate, because he needed a mindset to work on his skills and develop his craft. One could assume that Jerry wasn't interested in working on it. Maybe he believed in playing it loose, as "going lone wolf" had served him well in the past. It was also unfortunate that his management never asked what the hell he was presenting and how? (That's another story).

THE CRESCENDO SALES PITCH STRATEGY

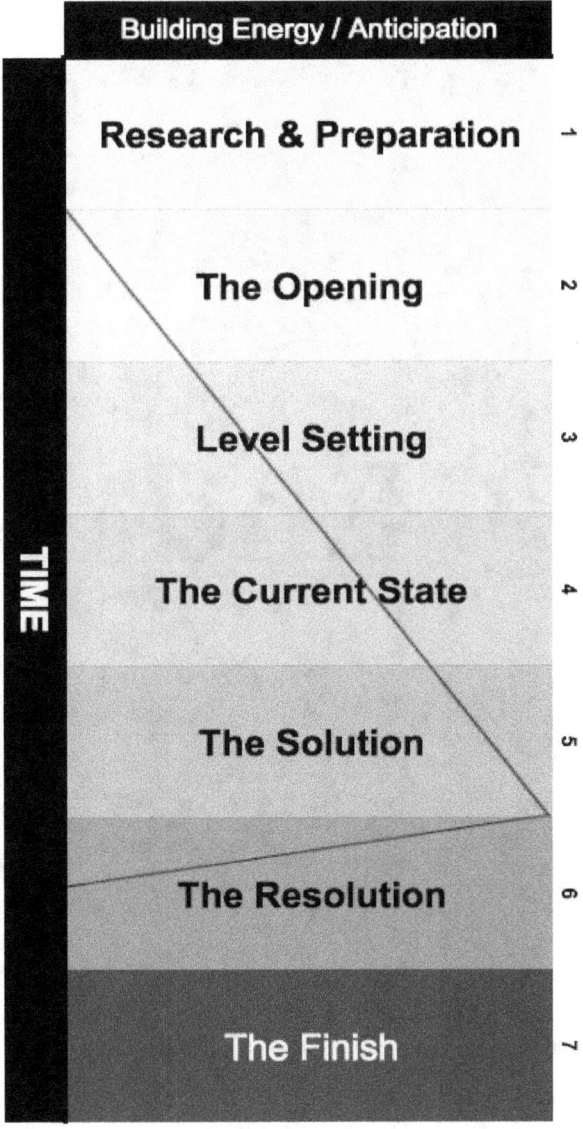

End

www.ingramcontent.com/pod-product-compliance
Lightning Source LLC
Chambersburg PA
CBHW070417220526
45466CB00004B/1444